MY WIFE'S GOING TO GET AWAY WITH MY MURDER

Cestius Gallus

ISBN-10:1976058996
ISBN-13:9781976058998

This book is dedicated to

David and Michelle Mercuri

"Big super fans"

AUTHOR'S MESSAGE

I am serious- I've been worried that my wife has been trying to kill me since 1995.

Don't let her get away with it!

In the words of our favorite corrupt NSW Detective "who needs proof when accusation will suffice"

Cestius Gallus ;)
XOXO

P.S email me at cestiusgallus@gmail.com

CONTENTS

BY LINCOLN HOUGHTON Esq

"Our love was a two person game.
At least until one of us died, and the
other became a murderer."

Dark Jar Tin Zoo.
Love quotes for the Ages.

"The rumor of my suicide is greatly
exaggerated, just wait a while and
the rumor of my murder may be
more truthful".

Cestius Gallus.
Great Australian True Crime Author.

"You need help dickhead, if I kill
you it's because I'm sick of you
telling everyone I'm plotting your
murder".

Cestius Gallus Wife.
Possible Future Convicted Murderer.

ACKNOWLEDGMENTS

Cestius Gallus would like to thank.

Ms Macey Mukow; *A terrific friend and family member who sadly passed away following a short and aggressive illness. She is forever in our hearts.*

Adam Davis

Brandon Nolan

Dr Oscar Sukit

Olivia and Luke Mercuri

Stephanie Purvis; *aka Ms X*

Deputy Sheriff Mr Brandan Holliday; *of the Adams County Sheriffs Department, Texas USA*

and the lovely Harry ;-)

NOTICE

All persons are innocent until proven guilty in a court of law, reader discretion is advised. This book is NOT intended to be used as a type of manual for evil minded women to kill their loving husbands.

The author does not condone the actions of his wife described in this book, the comments and views in this book are not necessarily shared by the author but are owned and the responsibility of his wife.

The author requests that the NSW Coroner conduct a full and wide ranging investigation if, I was found deceased or disappear. I'm not saying my wife has killed me, but let's just make sure she didn't.

NOTICE TO POLICE

This book is a fair and true account of the behavior displayed by the Author's wife, as observed and witnessed by the Author and others.

Further details regarding my wife's actions can be found in the yellow envelope marked "The bitch killed me" with a copy of my latest Will, a copy of my life insurance policy and details of reliable witnesses that is stored in the Author's safe deposit box held in the Author's Bank in Munich, Germany.

CHAPTER 1

PREMINITION OF MURDER

Just before we dive into the ultimate treacherous and murderous actions of my wife I would like to clarify for the record that I do not meet the criteria of suffering from the mental condition of paranoia. The condition of paranoia is described in the *Diagnostic and Statistical Manual of Mental Disorders of the American Psychiatric Association and the International Classification of Diseases* as a mental disorder known professionally as paranoid personality disorder. Sufferers of this very serious mental condition have a thought process that is heavily influenced by anxiety or fear, often to the point of delusion and irrationality.

Cestius Gallus is not afraid of anything and I do not suffer from anxiety. Due to the suspicious personality traits of paranoid people, they are usually single and cannot have interpersonal relationships and live very restricted lives. I have been happily married for many years and enjoy many friendships. I am a very social person with strong family interpersonal relationships. I am clearly not a paranoid person.

I said to Michael, my friend since 1999

"It is possible that my wife may kill me, she's smart so she will probably get away with it."

There are some people who believe that dreams can tell of future events, a premonition or warning of things that will occur. There are some people who earn a decent wage as they interpret dreams for others, as some dreams are so horrible that people seek an interpretation from professionals or gypsies.

It was the English psychologist A P Smyth that said,

"Dreams are the window to your future."

My dream started around August of 1995, my wife stared in my dream every night in a type of reoccurring horror movie. The dream was so realistic that I always woke sweating and out of breath as if I had just survived the horrible event.

My repetitive dream played this way;

I was seated in the lounge room watching the 6pm news on television and my wife is in the kitchen cooking dinner. She is dressed in a red apron and making pasta to her family's two hundred year old recipe. My wife is stirring a rich tomato sauce and she looks twice to see if I can see her, she reaches into the cupboard and removes a clear bowl with plastic wrap over it. My wife then dishes up the lovely pasta meal onto plates and the dream becomes more slow motion and black and white. Evil has come to my household. My wife picks up the bowl and now I become aware that it has the live bodies of spiders inside that she has cut the legs off using scissors. She emptied the spiders bodies onto my plate and stirs them into the pasta sauce. I wake up at this very moment of the dream.

I would regularly approach my wife and ask her if she was poisoning my food and she would become upset and would deny everything. Her strenuous denials would only serve to make me even more suspicious of her and she would become upset and refuse to talk to me for hours.

Just after the dreams started my wife would make a nice dinner and would want to sit and eat together under the romantic flickering lights of a scented candle at the dinner table. I admit now to the world that I was scared and would pick up my knife and fork and couldn't eat, not until I turned on the electric 60 watt light so I could see my food and hopefully detect any poison in my meal. It was stupid and dumb I know, that a person can't look at food and tell if it was poisoned or not. My friends tried to convince me that my wife probably didn't ever try to kill me through poisoning my food.

I saw a documentary on free to air television that mentioned about spider venom and to my horror, I discovered that Australia has three spiders that are able to kill a human with a single bite. I recalled my dream that plays every night, I fall asleep and tried to recall what type of spiders were in the bowl that my wife places into my food. I started to use a lot of surface spray around the house and even paid a pest controller to come to the house and spray the strongest chemicals allowed by law over every inch of my house. It was a type of fools belief that if I killed the spiders my wife wouldn't be able to kill me, of course she could always get spiders anywhere in Australia.

I examined my food before I ate, I discarded anything I was suspicious of and told everyone that would listen that my wife was probably trying to poison me. I wrote in my last will and testimony that I wanted a full toxicology examination of my body and for the Coroner to search for spider venom as a cause of death. I did not name my wife as my killer directly but my last will and testimony states;

"14:2:1 My death may have been caused by a person very close to me, so close that we share a bed and she is married to me"

In 1999, I became so paranoid about my wife poisoning my food with spiders that I telephoned the good people at the world famous Gosford Reptile Park, that is situated just North of Sydney. As part of the many functions of the park, they extract venom from snakes and spiders for medicines such as snake anti-venom and medical research. I spoke at length with a venom expert and to my horror I was informed that my wife could poison me by placing the bodies of live spiders in my food.

I remembered the famous words of Joseph Heller when he wrote in the script of the movie Catch 22;

 "Just because you're paranoid doesn't mean people aren't after you."

I was convinced in the cloud of my mind that my murder was going down just like this;

- My wife collects a number of live spiders and cuts off their little legs with a pair of scissors.

- My wife makes a meal, anything at all, and she simply puts the bodies of the spiders in my meal.

- I eat the spiders and then I DIE. She is a poor widow free to bring a date to my funeral. She escapes justice.

So now that I had worked out how my wife was planning to kill me with poison in my food, I wanted to know how she thought she would get away with the murder of her dear loving husband. I thought that the best way to deal with her trying to kill me was to just ask her directly, so I waited until dinner and after inspecting my salad and steak I asked "honey, how did you expect to get away with feeding me spiders?"

Now my wife is a calm and loving woman and she has put up with a lot of stupid things that I have done, but, when I asked her a direct question she exploded and yelled "you're a fucking fuckwad, I am not fucking feeding you fucking poison fuckwit! Now eat the fucking meal and shut the fuck up!"

The New South Wales Police Force teach new Detectives that when a suspect displays anger when replying to a direct question that the suspect is most probably avoiding the truth, and this is suspicious and needs follow up questions. I took a deep breath and I asked "please don't yell and stop avoiding the question. All I want to know is after you poison me what was the official story you were going to give the cops?" My wife became silent, she sat at the table and ate her meal while ignoring me and refusing to speak.

In Australia, we have the important common law right of silence and the privilege against self incrimination. There are some abrogations of the right, such as a witness giving evidence at a Royal Commission cannot refuse to answer a question. Under these rights, that are protected and upheld by the courts, my wife cannot be compelled to do anything or to speak about anything that will incriminate herself. My wife was smart enough that she was clearly protecting herself by maintaining her right of silence, and I respected her for that.

I wanted to show my loving wife that I was aware of her evil plan to murder me so I told her, "I know you want to place the bodies of spiders in my food, I know this, it's a fact!" She did not seem to be very amused and she gave me a serial killers glance and then continued eating her meal in complete silence. I continued, "I know that you have planned to remove the spider's legs and place their little bodies in my food." Again she sat in complete silence. I continued yet again, "all I want to know is how you plan on getting away with it?" Again my wife sat in silence.

Her diabolic plan to poison my food with live spiders was now fully exposed. Her evil, (husband killing genius plan) had been out witted by more then half as I figured out the method my wife was planning to end my life. The other parts of the unanswered questions are a mere detail, such as how was she planning on getting away with poisoning my food and the motive?

I sat drinking my coffee and pondering the two very important questions and the answers came to me between shop purchased chocolate chip cookies (because I no longer trusted her cooking).

- Motive; At this time the only possible motive for my wife murdering me is money. That ancient reason for a wife killing her husband has surfaced it's ugly head yet again, and my wife just wanted the life insurance money and our nest egg all to herself.

- My wife was planning to get away with using spiders venom to kill me. She could simply claim that I must have innocently ingested them while eating my meal.

- My loving wife would rely on her past three years of advanced acting lessons to appear like a grieving widow.

I was happy that now I had a lot of the pieces of this cunning bitch's evil plans. I sipped my coffee and reflected on what could have led the woman I had always seen as my beautiful and loving wife to wanting me dead. Was I such a horrible monster that the woman I fell in love with all those years ago would want me dead?

I also formed the suspicion that my wife would possibly create reasonable doubt to ensure she would get away with killing me. To do this she would memorize answers to typically asked questions by police so her responses would appear automatic and truthful. My evil hardhearted wife would use her advanced knowledge of police procedures and interrogation techniques, that she had gained observing and assisting me in writing true crime novels to her advantage and stay that single step ahead of the police.

My wife had devised a fool proof plan on how to kill me and get away with it so the manner of my death didn't matter as her plan to get away with it was universal. "This bitch is good" I whispered just under my breath to myself and my fear was again fully restored.

The following day I spoke to many people about the evil plan of my loving wife to kill me. I told them about her motive, her method and how she would get away with it, most people just dismissed me as paranoid and one friend said, "you're a nut job."

At 6pm my wife called me and our kids to the dinner table for a meal of pasta. I became hyper alert to my surroundings as a sense of Déjà Vu overtook my mind and body. This was exactly the same in every way to my reoccurring dream, this was the moment my wife murders me. I thought that having the advanced warning of my reoccurring dream and the evidence I had collected since August 1995, that I could change the outcome of the evil plans of my loving and caring wife.

I stood and casually walked into the kitchen, I checked the garbage bin and noticed that she had already emptied it into the outside council bin for collection the next morning. I became very worried as my wife had cleared away all evidence that could have incriminated her, she would know that the police would want to collect and inspect the containers of the food that my wife had prepared for my last meal. My wife was one step ahead of the police and had cleared the kitchen waste for collection in the morning by the council that would take place hours before she would have to report my death.

I knew now I was a marked man, and that this was the night my dream comes true. I returned to the dining table and thought that this was my last meal on earth unless I can do something to change my fate. I asked my cunning wife, "babe, why did you take the rubbish outside to the wheelie bin?" and she replied in a slightly raised voice, "because you're a lazy asshole and someone had too." I had nothing in reply to that statement.

My wife had thought this out well and can even claim that the food was already contaminated by the manufacturer with spiders. In this modern age a lot of foods come from countries that have less stringent food safety and quality control legislation then Australia. This would allow her to use the old reasonable doubt creation to escape a murder charge and could, if the court accepted, that the food may have been contaminated by the manufacturer.

My wife would be free to take legal action against the food manufacturer and seek millions of dollars in compensation. Add these millions to my three life insurance policies of similar value (that my loving wife insisted on me having) and our $3,500 nest egg savings in the bank and this evil bitch of a wife is sitting pretty on a yacht in the sea of murder.

I turned my attention back to my wife and became aware that the murderer had taken advantage of my searching the kitchen bin for confirmation of her treachery, and that my beautiful wife had dished out and placed the meals on the table. I was nervous and I said, "babe, let's swap seats for tonight, we can mix it up a little, it'll be fun" and she replied in an automatic manner, "no I like sitting here, eat your dinner before it gets cold."

Now I have found myself in a serious situation. I thought that if I suggest to the wife that I swap places with one of our kids, that she would stop it happening if the meal in front of me has been poisoned. I asked my eldest daughter if she wanted to sit in daddy's spot at the table. She looked at me and said, "no, I don't want to eat that penne daddy." Now I was a second away from panic and calling the police and then my youngest asked, "can I mummy, I want to swap with daddy." My loving wife said, "I don't care, just hurry up, you're all bloody crazy tonight." I knew from that moment I was safe to eat that night and I eagerly sat and ate my pasta and even commented at it's better then usual taste.

The next day I spoke to my friend Michael, "mate, I'm sure I've worked out that my wife is going to poison my food with spiders and she's thought it through in a cunning and smart way." Michael laughed and asked what did I mean. I explained, "she's going to do it on bin night, the wrappers from the food she cooks will be cleared away and collected by the council."

He looked in blank amazement so I continued, "the wrappers are evidence. She is going to get rid of the evidence before the cops are called, I think she'll sue the food manufacturer after she beats the murder charge." Michael then said, "you're mad, she loves you, why would she want you dead?" I didn't know how to answer his question, so I asked him, "do you think she needs a reason not to kill me?"

My dreams continued and were exactly the same

night after night. I read an article on dreams called *Deja Vu and Dreams Really Coming True* that featured on exemplore.com, that scared me even more. The article validated my fears and made the threat against me very much real.

My thoughts that my wife was trying to kill me grew stronger and was starting to effect my life in every way. As we were driving to her parents house I took advantage of her being stuck in a moving car and asked her, "honey, I've worked out how you're going to poison me. I worked out how your going to easily create reasonable doubt, I think I've worked out how your going to make my death pay millions for you. I just don't know why babe, why do you want me dead? Like it's gotta be more then money, have I wronged you?"

Well I've receive a few bravery medals in my life for having the courage to act when other people run in fear and I can tell you right now that I cringed in fear at her reply. "Asshole, I'm going to tell you again, I'm not going to kill you! If you ask me anything about this shit again, I'll force feed you rat bait as a fucking suppository after I cut your cock off" and the look of pure hatred on her face, was enough for me to know that the once loving wife I had devoted myself to was now a woman scorned and my days were numbered. There is an old saying;

"Hell knows no fury like a woman scorned"

I stopped asking my wife questions about what I knew to be true and I did not want to provoke her into killing me before I could take the necessary steps to prevent her evil. I started being more romantic towards my wife. I can assure you that I am a notoriously romantic man and it is hard to escalate the romance when your operating at such a high level. I was convinced that I was going to make my wife fall back in love with me again and hopefully she would abandon her plans to poison me. Plans that I am sure that you would agree she denies so as to not incriminate herself.

In early 2005, my reoccurring dream suddenly stopped and I was denied any dreams in my sleep. I began to relax and began to eat my wife's cooking without the worry of her poisoning me. Still to this very day as a lingering psychological hangover I have to eat with the lights on but without the gripping fear that the next meal I have will be my last. It appeared to me that my efforts to expose my loving wife's evil plan had worked and she had abandoned her efforts to kill me.

CHAPTER 2

THE FIRST REAL ATTEMPT

In the early part of February 2010, I woke in the middle of the night sweating and short of breath. I had a nightmare, but incredibly for the first time in about five years I had an actual dream. My dream was horrific and seemed very realistic, like an action movie being played in 3D and my wife and I were the only actors. I looked over at the clock and I noticed the smile on my wife's face as she slept, I realized that the dream was warning me that she was at her evil ways again and wanted me dead.

Dreams can be your minds subconscious, conveying a warning of dangers that you face according to Naomi Goodlet the author of Dreams - Messages from your Subconscious. Naomi sets out a very sensible argument that your minds subconscious causes you to dream of dangers that are real in an attempt to warn you.

A very good friend of mine is also a great and well respected Doctor and Psychiatrist in Europe. He is one of the worlds leading criminal psychiatrists. We first became friends when we worked on a project to assist the teenage victims of bullying, and whenever he is in Australia he makes sure he visits. Since I have been writing the champion novels that you all love to read, my friend Dr Oscar Sukit has often advised me on the psychological aspects of the criminal mind. I needed help to understand the mind of a homicidal and manipulative spousal killer and knew that the good Doctor was only a phone call away.

I rang Dr Sukit at his Berlin office in Germany, and explained the entire events and what evidence I had collected to date on my wife with him. My friend sat quietly and actively listened and then told me in his most professionally soft and calming voice,

"You are aware, that I know you are talking about your wife? A person I know well and call my friend, the same as I call you my friend. I cannot comment on such matters involving her."

His words sounded to me that my wife had gotten to my friend before I did, and she had successfully manipulated him. Dr Sukit added, "Cestius, I know of a peer of mine that you could talk with, I think your PTSD is showing it's head again." I politely declined his offer to organize a meeting with his peer, as I would prefer to find someone that my wife and Dr Sukit could not have contaminated.

It was late January 2012, and I had the same horror dream every night for two years. I conducted some research on the power of dreams, and if there was any evidence at all that they were a premonition of the future. I purchased a book titled *"Chicken Soup for the Soul: Dreams and Premonitions"* written by Amy Newmark and Kelly Sullivan Walden. The book only fueled the fire of suspicion that burnt inside me and I knew that my wife was again trying to kill me. It is very concerning to know that your subconscious mind has identified that my wife was at her old tricks, and was focused on killing me and there is nothing that you can do as no one will act on a dream of a PTSD suffering husband with no tangible evidence to present to a Judge.

The Sydney weather was fairly typical for summer and my wife and I decided that we should buy a second hand motor vehicle. I took her to the many car yards on Sydney's Parramatta Road. My wife and I strolled around the vehicles and she soon found interest in a Mitsubishi Pajero wagon that was white in color and ran on unleaded petrol. Interestingly most people are unaware that the word Pajero means wanker in the Spanish language.

My wife sat in the drivers seat and examined the car in detail, she looked up the Australian Governments ANCAP safety rating on her smart phone. She then questioned at length the second hand car salesman about the strength of the steel bull bar fitted to the front of the vehicle. I remember thinking, "what the fuck is she on about" when my wife commented that she wanted airbags for safety and this car had only one fitted on the driver's side.

My wife seemed very interested in the safety of the motor vehicle and I was very proud of her for being a savvy shopper for such an important asset. The car salesman was taken back by her online research and intense questioning by my wife, and he started the price negotiation at fifteen hundred dollars lower then the original asking price.

My wife took a strong position in the negotiation process and I stood like a puppet in the corner, while my wife screwed the poor car salesman into agreeing to a price so low that he was going to be eating two minute noodles for dinner all of next week. We drove away with a great looking and mechanically sound four wheel drive at a great price. My wife purchased one of those seat belt cushions for herself, and spent many hours cleaning the cars interior with a special cleaner and sun protector that left the dashboard a little slippery but very clean.

My wife surprised me even more when she had an LED spotlight fitted to the bull bar and a CB radio. I loved how my wife drove the car everywhere and how much of an interest she took in the four wheel drive. I saw my wife becoming a redneck hillbilly and even thought that any day she would come home with a gun rack and shotgun while chewing tobacco and wearing those little denim shorts.

My wife reminded me that she came from a long line of fruit traders, and that they know how to bash a deal so hard that the seller is happy to almost give away the item simply to get you out of their store. This demonstrated the shear cunning and sneakiness of the woman that I had married.

It was around a month after buying the car, and in hindsight I recall my wife strongly suggesting that we travel to a country location in the Riverina of New South Wales. She claims that I had input into the decision to drive to the lovely Riverina, however, I am sure I just went along with her suggestions because I didn't care where we went. I packed a great picnic basket and blanket for the day and as we were just about to set off my wife insisted on driving on our big country drive.

We stopped at some little shitty one horse town that would have been better named "Allfirstcousins" that is just near West Wyalong, *(if you have ever been there, you just know what I mean)* as we needed fuel. This sounds horrible to state such adverse things about a small country town, however, written in large black letters on the only unleaded fuel bowser was the sentence *"don't put this stuff in diesel cars."*

Now how is someone supposed to think about the people who live in this small town of about a hundred people or so when you read that? To quote my wife who read the sentence, "what type of backward hicks live here when they can read that sentence but cannot understand not to put unleaded fuel I a diesel car?" I am not in any way associated with or paid by Tourism New South Wales, but you just have to take a drive into some of these small areas of New South Wales and see for yourself these funny locations.

We were soon back on the open road and found ourselves on the Newell Highway, that is actually a pot hole riddled goat track and no way to the standards of an important rural highway. My wife took an unscheduled turn, and sped along this nameless long and dusty dirt country road with a surprisingly dangerous posted speed limit of 100 km/h. The road was made of dirt and some rocks and very large trees were suspiciously close to the edge of the road. My wife never exceeded 90 km/h as she powered down a road that would have made me feel safer if she did not exceed 50 km/h.

I asked my loving and beautiful wife, "sweetheart, where are we going? There looks like nothing is down here?" as I glanced around the area seeing nothing, not even a crow. There was a crop of wheat on the left of the road and on the right side was a paddock full of the most boring sheep you ever saw in your life. I am talking so boring that the editor of this book made me take out the three paragraphs I wrote that described the sheep.

Now I know that I am the clear victim of treachery and attempted murder, and that my version of what happened next would reasonably differ to the other parties. In this case, the other party is my loving wife and the mother of my children and my version is only very slightly different to the version that my loving wife tells to our family and friends.

My wife's version of her lies and deceit that she told to her parents in my presence just days after the accident;

"I was driving along the road because the people at the truck stop told me that halfway along the road is a farm, where the man sells antiques from his farm gate and fresh farm eggs. When I approached a bend in the road, the cars tires lost all grip in the bull dust layer on the road top surface and we span out of control and then the car turned over. I was so scared and screamed as it turned over a few times and finally, just after I saw my entire life flash before my eyes and I thought how I wouldn't see my husband and kids again, the car came to rest on it's roof. Thanks to God we were unhurt. Amen."

The raw truth of the event and her evil attempt on my life, is so much different to the horrible lies as told by my wife. The raw truth on what happened that day can best be described as a heinous, deliberate and treacherous attempted murder on my life.

This is the honest and painful truth of the near deadly event as told by me to my long time friend Michael, without exaggeration or alteration;

"the air was clean and fresh with a slight southerly breeze, as my wife drove down the dangerous twisty gravel road at 90 km/h with reckless abandoned. I was nervous, the same type of nervous you see in the eyes of a Catholic alter boy after church, as she sped towards nothing as if she was running late for an important appointment.

There seemed to be no reason for being on this road at all, as my wife appeared focused on her driving and kept sneaking looks in her rear vision mirror as if checking to ensure we were not being followed. The dust of the road was kicked up from the speed of the tyres, and formed a visually impregnable barrier to the sight of any onlookers.

I saw a sweeping dog's leg bend in the road up ahead, that was clearly sign posted and appeared to look as the most dangerous bend on this road to nowhere. I became concerned, as she did not remove her foot from the accelerator and sped towards the bend with no concern for the safety of myself in any noticeable manner.

We entered the middle of the bend at an outrageous

90 km/h with my wife's foot firmly planted on the accelerator and showing no signs of her slowing the car or using the breaks. The car swerved from side to side and then without warning I saw a very large tree ahead of me, and I felt the car roll over and over many times. I recall with great fear and detail the windscreen smashing and watching in a kind of slow motion, as I was showered in glass that appeared to reflect the suns peaceful and warming rays.

My attention could not focus on any particular happening, as the sunroof exploded inwards as the heavy vehicle tumbled in the most unnatural manner that was accompanied by the grievous sounds of violence and twisting metal. I reached out with my left arm to grab the dashboard support bar to steady myself, and at this time the car struck something that I could only guess as a large solid object and I felt my body change direction in this awful and terrifying event.

A large branch of a gum tree penetrated the roof just above my head tearing a foot long gash in the steel roof of the car, the wood of the tree somehow missing my head and killing me. I must have blacked out when the collapsing roof struck my head with great force as the car rolled for what I think was the fourth time.

When I became conscious again it was surreal, as I could no longer feel the violent twisting and turning of the accident and yet I felt strangely safe as I could feel the suns warmth on the side of my face. I became aware that I was suspended in my seat upside down, and that my mouth was filled with the taste of blood and I was now missing a tooth from the rear of my mouth.

I was flooded with great fear for the safety of my wife, and I struggled with pain as I turned my head towards the driver's seat only to become instantly aware of her serial killer gaze that was aimed towards me. I became scared that maybe she had deliberately caused the accident to kill me, yes she was cold and cunning, staging an accident to kill me.''

The near enough scientific and forensic facts of the accident that cannot be disputed became known to me after my recovery from the accident;

1. The road is notoriously dangerous and there had been a recent death along the road. Numerous signs and warning notices are posted along the road by the local government.

2. The tragic road death was reported in a newspaper that is local to that area and was also published online. I knew that my wife

had access to the internet at her place of residence, on her mobile smart phone, via wifi at any of the millions of free wifi providers in Australia. Also at any number of internet cafe's in New South Wales, and could have looked at the newspaper article and as she had access to the newspaper article she would have known the road was dangerous.

3. My wife's airbag deployed and protected her from any injury. My wife had insisted on a driver's side airbag, and knew the car was not fitted with an airbag on the passenger's side. My loving wife had even checked the ANCAP safety rating, and knew the passenger would be protected only by God and luck and the standard seat belt.

4. The seat belt cushion she had purchased for the driver's side, had protected her from the normal bruises that are sustained in these types of accidents from the seat belt. My wife had deliberately not purchased the passenger's side seat belt one of those cushions.

5. My loving wife had made sure that I was seated in the passenger's seat for the accident by insisting that she drove the

vehicle. Her cunning and manipulative ways almost worked, almost.

I was grateful that my wife was miraculously uninjured and was alive. As I struggled to free myself from the smoking wreckage that remained twisted on the roadway, I became alarmed at the ease of my wife to exit the motor vehicle and how she did not come to my assistance. Bleeding and unable to think properly, I finally exited the car and rolled onto the rough and dirty surface of the road.

My loving wife was silent for what seemed like minutes and when she finally spoke all she said was, "I can't believe that I ruined my car." I am not a paranoid man and I am not a man that jumps easily to accuse a person of the most heinous of crimes that can be committed in our modern society and yet I suspected, on reasonable grounds, that my wife wanted me dead. Had it not been for the actions of God's divine intervention I would not have survived her latest attempt on my life.

A normal person would display concern for their loved ones that are injured in a terrible and violent motor vehicle accident. Your typical wife and mother would normally ask their husband of many years if they were alive and if they need assistance to get out of a motor vehicle. My wife said in a very melancholy voice, "I can't believe that I ruined my car." It was abundantly clear to me that my survival had flustered my wife and she simply couldn't bring herself to show any type of concern for my well being.

I spoke to my friend Michael again, "I'm sure she staged the accident to kill me!" He answered without a moments pause to ponder the gravity of my statement, "you're fucking nuts, she's not trying to kill you." I then went through the facts of this story in great detail in an attempt to convince Michael of my wife's evil actions. I can confirm with great sadness, that his position on this matter did not change and he believed that my wife was innocent.

I contacted a long term fan of my true crime novels who lives in the United States of America, Deputy Sheriff Mr Brandan Holliday. He is a Deputy Sheriff in Adam County, and an expert in the science of traffic collisions and vehicle accident investigations. I believed that if I could prove the car accident was staged in an attempt to kill me, then I would have the evidence that would convince people that my life was in danger. We chatted for many hours and he had me return to the scene of the alleged crime and take photographs and record measurements of the evidence that remains.

After Deputy Sheriff Mr Brandan Holliday had

examined all the evidence I had sent him, his professional conclusion was that my wife was traveling at the speed I recalled and that it was most likely a combination of over correcting of the steering and heavy breaking that was the cause of the accident. In simple talk, "human action caused the accident" or to use my own words "alleged failed attempted murder."

When I showed the evidence to my friends and family they all dismissed my hypotheses as "ridiculous," and posed the already answered three million dollar question of "why would she murder you?"

My wife is very clever and knows her rights at law. She would not be easily fooled into a confession, and I knew that she can only be destroyed with evidence. I had a momentary flashback to a conversation I had with her only months before the accident where she stated, "criminals are so dumb! All you have to do is keep your mouth shut and never assist the police." As I recalled her words I now thought about what sort of law abiding citizen would even think that way and the answer was simple, only a criminally minded black widow is who.

Murder disguised as a car accident. It seemed that my beautiful and loving wife had again tried to kill me and finally, I had a little real physical evidence to prove that she was Australia's next evil black widow killer. My wife had waited many years after her last evil plan to kill me had failed, and now after the dust had settled and the thoughts of her trying to kill me had faded in the memories of everyone I had told of her last plan. She had given it one more good attempt. Part of me thought that I would be safe now for a little while and part of me thought that it was now going to be harder to stop her as she has clearly become a more sophisticated killer.

It is a universally accepted fact that serial killers evolve their skills and knowledge. The typical serial killer's first murder is usually where they make their biggest mistakes, and they the become better killers and smarter at evading capture through experience. It did enter my mind that my wife was only going to get better with every attempt on my life, and that if I did not stop her then I would be dead before my children finish high school. The haunting sound of the clock ticking down on my life was ever present and I am determined to stop her getting away with my murder.

When you consider that my wife had gone to such lengths to ensure that she would be relatively safe in a high speed motor vehicle accident and I would be more vulnerable to fatal injury as a passenger, the conclusion is even more sinister and evil. The premeditation of her evil actions made the crime and attack even more heinous. My wife had undertaken great research into the vehicles safety features and capabilities and with the power of hindsight I said aloud, "she had planned to kill me from the first day we went car shopping, the same as if she had planned to plunge a knife in my heart."

I contacted my friend and colleague Dr Sukit Sukit, and again shared the facts and anecdotal evidence on the numerous attempts on my life and he said;

"Cestius, the car accident could have been innocent and you are looking into this in a way that you are trying to find sinister actions on behalf of your wife."

He was now dead to me. I didn't even say goodbye when I terminated the telephone conversation.

How much time had my wife invested to convince so many people that she is above suspicion, when the entire time she has been fully committed to killing me for a few penny's. Amongst pedophiles is a shared trait known as grooming. It is where the evil men, *(unfortunately it is generally men who commit these horrors)* spend long periods of time convincing people that they are honest and good citizens, when all the time they are monsters that sexually assault children. I'm not saying that my wife is a pedophile, I am saying that she had obviously groomed our family and friends into believing that she is a role model wife and that butter wouldn't melt in her mouth. My wife must have invested a long period of time grooming Dr Sukit, and convinced him that she was above any suspicions or allegations that could be aimed at her.

I am not a stupid man, and I had been listening to the constant words of everyone around me that I must be paranoid. So I made an appointment with a local psychologist. I wanted there to be a cloak of secrecy around the appointment, so my wife was not aware of who I was seeing and what for. I believed that if she knew what I was doing she would somehow try and manipulate or persuade this professional into making an incorrect diagnosis the same as she had done with Dr Oscar Sukit.

My first appointment was for an hour and when I first walked into the room I used my most authoritarian voice and demanded, *"I want to be tested to see if I suffer from paranoid personality disorder or anything like it."* The psychologist was the consummate professional, and took more then the first appointment to confidently give me their most accurate professional diagnosis. The psychologist's report was four and a half pages long and cost me almost $1,900. I read with a happy heart in the summery of the report that stated in clear language;

"there is no evidence of the patient suffering from the mental condition of paranoid personality disorder or any other disorder of a similar nature."

There you have it! "I am fucking in your face sane, you bunch of non believer assholes." I yelled out way too loud for my own liking, and displaying a hint of my post traumatic stress disorder showing its ugly face again.

Feelings of vindication were strong and I had now proven beyond any doubt that I was not a paranoid man in any way, making my suspicions and the circumstantial evidence more believable. I was now armed with a lot of circumstantial evidence, a little physical evidence and proof that I am not some paranoid person seeing danger in every place.

I could now conclude with great confidence that I am a dead man walking, and through either divine intervention or shear luck the evil plots of my cunning stone hearted wife had failed twice. It's the same as somehow the coyote always fails to kill the road runner in the cartoons that I used to watch when I was a kid.

Unfortunately, when I presented the evidence that I am not a paranoid person to my friends and family it was dismissed and they continued with their objections that I am married to a killer. I did not know what to do, if I couldn't gain their support and convince them that I was married to this evil monster then how could I convince a narrow minded police officer who only knows how to investigate the theft of a child's bicycle from a garden shed.

I now found myself often considering if I should kill her before she kills me. Please understand that as a former law enforcement officer and a man of high morals and integrity, it is not easy to entertain such thoughts. I suppose the thoughts were powered mainly by the lack of support from my family and friends, as no one believed that my wife was trying to kill me. Everyone is telling me that I do not have enough evidence to approach the police and that I would be laughed at. So I had to consider that the only course of action is to get her before she gets me. The law of the jungle would have to prevail in this battle between man and wife.

I asked myself if I could actually choke the life from this bitch to save my own life, and my heart screamed at me that love will prevail and that I could win her over with romance as I couldn't bring myself to hurting her. Hurting my wife would also hurt my children and that was unacceptable, even at the cost of my own life.

CHAPTER 3

WHAT'S HER MOTIVE?

In Australia, it not necessary to prove the motive of murderers in a court of law. To secure a conviction the police only have to prove that a person has done the act of killing another person without a legal justification. A lawful killing in Australia is very hard to prove in a court as the person, regardless of who they are, that actually does the killing must prove that their life or the life of another person is in immediate and grave and immediate danger. Clearly I did not have enough evidence to convince a court of law that I could legally kill my wife or have her charged with my attempted murder.

I formed the theory that if I could identify the motive of my wife to kill me, and somehow remove that motive from causing the temptation or necessity for her to murder her loving and devoted husband then I will be safe. My friend Deputy Sheriff Mr Brandan Holliday asked me, "what would be her motive to kill you?" and I did not want to answer the question straight away.

I sat on my veranda and sipped a soy latte as I nursed my injuries from the car accident, I thought very hard about what could be the motive of my darling wife to undertake the most heinous of crimes against me.

I discussed the latest events and my newly formed theory at our local pub with my friend Michael and he commented, "mate if your wife really hated you, why wouldn't she just leave you?" I replied without even thinking, "this bitch is after money. If she leaves me then she gets nothing, a few bucks for child support and not another cent." Michael was still not convinced that my wife was plotting to kill me and soon the topic of conversation changed to discussing the practical uses of the big breasts on the bar maid.

It was very hard to fight the thoughts that maybe I should kill her before she kills me. A kind of kill or be killed event that exists mainly on the battlefield for soldiers, and on the mean streets for police and law enforcement agents. My heart is screaming out no you can't, whilst inside my head and my ever sensible mind is still considering all options and one of those is to kill or be killed.

I remember the poem, The law for the Wolves written by Rudyard Kipling and the passage;

"ye may kill for yourselves, and your mates, and your cubs as they need and ye can;
But kill not for pleasure of killing, and seven times never kill man."

My wife must have a motive to kill me. I was heart broken as I have endlessly romanced her with an honest and loving heart since we met and yet we are at this crossroad on the highway of pure hatred and evil. "I must discover her motive and stop her." I said aloud for all of the universe to hear.

As if I was writing another champion true crime novel, I dove into research and examined the typical motives for females to murder. I read the work of Robi Ludwig, the co-author of "Til Death Do Us Part" and also examined a document by the Australian Institute of Criminology (AIC), titled Motives for Homicide, published in November 2005. The AIC document placed domestic argument as the highest female motive for murder and Robi Ludwig, confirmed that a female is most likely to commit murder if her needs are not met such as during an argument. I ruled this motive out as I had not had any significant argument with my wife since we had been married and we both had a pact never to go to bed angry with each other. Something that she clearly did not follow as she was trying to murder me. I was reminded by my dear friend Mrs Macey Mukow;

"A sane man cringes when a woman is scorned."

The only issue is that I did not think that my dear wife was a woman scorned, only a killer waiting to strike. Mrs Mukow said, "if she is trying to kill you darling, she is a woman scorned." I simply could not find any reason that would support the statement that my wife was a woman scorned.

Money and drugs is another solid typical motive of females for murder as supported by the AIC statistics. My wife had a very right wing view to drug users and she wouldn't even take paracetamol for a headache, I could rule out drugs very quickly. My wife once said, "drug addicts and drug dealers need to have their hands cut off, then the community can clearly see who is a shitbag."

Money became top of the list for motive, as I recalled in great detail how my wife had taken over the financial situation of the household. It was after one day in 2015, when I came home from the shops with a new laptop computer and a LED television without consulting her, or paying the bills before I splashed out on what she referred to as luxuries. Since then she had demanded receipts from me and checked our bank account every day with an app on her smart phone.

My wife always made sure that she had paid my life insurance policies on time and in full. Regardless of what I think, she maintained three separate policies that all named her as the sole beneficiary of any and all payouts on my death. I checked my files and discovered that the combined total of the policies equaled around three million dollars on my death. I know I had around $3,500 in our joint bank savings account and then there was my superannuation policy that was pumped full of money by the New

South Wales Government when I was employed by them for all those many years. Money appears to be the most obvious reason for my wife wanting me dead.

I emailed a friend and fanatical fan of my true crime novels, a person known to me as Stephanie Purvis. *(she actually requested that I could call her Ms X)* She is a student of law at one of Sydney's best University and inquired about the history of "black widow killers" in Australia.

She described a black widow killer as one who is;

"a woman who is married to or in a significant personal relationship with a man that she kills for money or a benefit."

I did not want to think immediately that the mother of my children had fitted the typical psychological profile of a black widow killer, however, I was not prepared to rule out anything when it came to stopping this evil bitch from killing me. The reality is that if my wife's motive was money then she was indeed an evil black widow killer.

I decided to bring Stephanie into my confidence and told her the horrible story of deceit and the treacherous attempts on my life at the hands of my darling wife. Stephanie was so alarmed by the story, that she advised me to "go and talk with the police and to take your suspicions to them. They will protect you and basically save the lives of your children."

My children! now that was a thought I had not considered. Would this evil and cunning rat of a wife actually kill my children? The short answer was simply no. The long answer was, when I weighed up all the evidence I realized that she could have easily ensured the children were in the motor vehicle at the time of the accident. I could immediately dismiss the thought of my darling and loving wife killing our well behaved and great children. If I am honest with myself I will admit that with being able to dismiss the threat towards my children, then I was filled with the chilling realization that I must be the only target of this sweet assassin.

My friend and confidant of almost fifteen years Mr Adam Davis, was consulted over a few drinks and he asked;

"what makes you so important that they will call your murder an assassination?."

What a question to be asked, how do you answer that question without looking like a vein moron? I do like to think that I am important to my children and a few friends, but he was right? After I answer the question of why my wife wants to murder me, I would have to examine inside myself if I was important enough to be assassinated or just simply murdered.

Was my wife an assassin or a murderer? The answer exists only in my real life importance. I told Adam, "We will have to revisit this at a later time. For now I will have to concentrate on proving that my wife has a motive to kill me." The question remained with me for many weeks as I examined every part of my life.

I rang my famous researcher and investigator Benjamin, and asked him to run a full background check on my wife. He asked, "what am I looking for?" and I told him, "I really don't know much about her life before I met her. I only know what little she has told me. Find out everything about her since she was born until the day I married her."

The game was afoot, and now I would soon have the upper hand and be able to foil the evil plot of my loving wife to kill me. My researcher Benjamin is excellent and very thorough, and after just a few days of him tearing down the dark barriers of my wife's past we met at a cafe in Malabar, where he reported to me on his initial findings on my wife.

Benjamin reported;

- My wife was born on the 28th July in Ryde

Hospital in Sydney's North West at 23:25hrs *(11:25pm)* to the parents Anne and Tony.

- Both parents are recorded in the hospitals documents and on her birth certificate.

- My wife was delivered shortly after arrival at the hospital by Dr Michael H Davenport who was on duty at the hospital at the time.

- My wife was christened at Saint Charles church in Sydney's North West and her God parents are her aunt and uncle who she is now estranged from.

- My loving wife attended the primary school just around the corner from her family home where she became a Library Monitor when in year five.

- My wife enjoyed ballet dancing as a child and played soccer on the weekends. She also undertook swimming as a sport before school commenced for many years where she earnt many tropheys and certificates for her excellent swimming abilities.

- My wife attended a private Catholic High School where she was a slightly above average student. She was voted a peer support student and appeared to be a popular girl with the other students. Her Head mistress who is a Nun of the catholic Church confirmed that she had a pleasant disposition and was keen to excel in her studies.

- During her high school years she had three boyfriends. Although I will not name the boys in this book, Benjamin noticed that all three boys had similarities and styles that are similar to my own.

My wife's taste in men, as impeccable as they are, had not changed since she started High School. Benjamin and myself both agree that in life there is no such thing as a coincidence, and these old high school boyfriends were of interest for the unusual coincidence that existed.

I asked Benjamin, "these boyfriends, could you find out why they broke up with her? Or anything about them?" and he replied, "mate steady yourself for this, I can't overlook the facts" and then as he told me about these men I am sure that I could have been knocked down with a feather, as the obvious coincidence was so overwhelming and alarming that I just simply could not ignore it.

Her first high school boyfriend is now deceased. He died in a car accident only five years after being the boyfriend of my wife. The Police report was short and the facts are not fully known about his accident, except that he was fatally injured when the vehicle he was a passenger in left the roadway and struck a tree in a semi rural road in Sydney's southwest. My wife was the driver, yes that is an obvious coincidence that one cannot overlook. My wife had a car accident and her boyfriend was killed in almost the identical circumstances that exist when she rolled our four wheel drive and I was almost killed.

"Hang on a moment" I was taken back by the facts unearthed by Benjamin. "Did you just say that my wife was the driver of the car?" Benjamin confirmed the facts and I said, "doesn't it strike you as unusual that my wife has never mentioned that she has killed a man before?" Benjamin then said in his usual calm voice, "mate, would you tell your wife that you have killed someone? She may not have told you because, she is still carrying great guilt or sorrow and we all know you wouldn't have married her because of it."

I quickly blurted out of my mouth to Benjamin, how it was about five years after I had foiled my wife's plans to poison me that the car accident happened. Benjamin read me a copy of the coroners report and although he looked into the fatality as much as is humanly possible, he could find nothing suspicious about the accident. "Just like the accident my wife had staged, in that bitches attempt to kill me." I stated a little louder then I intended.

The second high school boyfriend of my wife is currently single and friends with my wife on Facebook. My researcher Benjamin was able to discover that he had presented to Nepean Hospital whilst he was in high school with a suspected case of severe food poisoning, after eating Indian take away food. Now that coincidence is just mind blowing when compared with what I am alleging has been happening in my own household.

The last boyfriend my wife had in high school is living only 500 meters from my home. He is married with one child, and somehow my loving wife has never told me these facts. Benjamin ascertained that this boyfriend is fully aware of my wife's residence, and yet no evidence can be found that the two have communicated in any way since his moving to the local area. I would think about this for many nights wondering why my wife has never told me about her ex boyfriend living 500 meters away from us.

I was shocked at this initial report and Benjamin added; "your wife attended a business college in Parramatta, and has worked at her current employer since leaving the college." Other then the unusual coincidence between her past boyfriends and the attempts on my own life, there did not seem to be anything else in her past to raise suspicion or that could be used to prove that she was an evil spousal killer that was hell bent on murdering her loving husband.

Benjamin dropped a bomb on me when he said, "I took it that you suspect your wife of adultery or something. So, I placed a GPS tracker on her car and installed spy software on her phone that I lifted when I was at your house last time." Benjamin had mistaken my request to find out some background information on my wife because I suspect she is trying to kill me, as I was suspecting she was not faithful.

I clarified my real intentions on having the information for him and he asked, "I have the records who she is contacting, do you want to know about it?" I told him that I thought this was a total invasion of her privacy and I did not agree with these spying methods but, I needed to hear this.

My wife had been text messaging her mother and her sappy, boring and bland friends, *(I am not a fan of my wife's friends especially Alyssa)* and she had called me every morning and afternoon without failure for about four minutes at a time. She has been driving from our home to the railway station where she catches a train to work, and then in the afternoon she drove back home via the kids school when she picked them up.

Her daily routine was not suspicious and yet it was evidence of a cool character with nothing untoward in their life who had only money as a motive for killing their devoted and loving husband. Benjamin stated, "there is only this strange routine that is repeated every Monday to Friday without fail."

Benjamin pointed out that the only break in my wife's routine was two days ago, she also stopped for about five minutes at a service station where she fueled her car. Benjamin said, "I'm sorry to pry but are you sure? Your wife seems pretty devoted to you, do you have any evidence?" I almost sacked him on the spot for questioning me about this, but I decided to lay the evidence out for him and let him make up his own mind about this cold and evil black widow killer masquerading as my loving and caring wife.

I couldn't just tell my wife I knew about her killing an old boyfriend in a near identical circumstances to her attempt on my life, as she would be alerted to my prying into her background. I did need to know why she had kept it from me and it did add to the growing evidence against her. I needed to think about how I would have her confess that she had been responsible for killing before, and then I can confront her in a more aggressive manner about her attempts to kill me. This was giving me a constant headache, and I felt that killing her before she kills me was not my best option right now as soon I would have this black widow in an iron cage for life.

A few weeks later I again met with my researcher Benjamin, and I again went through the entire saga where my wife was trying to poison my food and the evil plot of my wife to kill me by staging a car accident. I asked Benjamin for his advice and input as to how I could best prove my accusation. Benjamin sat very quiet and finally said, "really, the bitch!" with his simple and short sentence I believed that I had convinced the most competent and skeptical investigator in Australia, of my wife's evil intentions and I asked, "do you think I have enough to go to the police?" and he said, "no mate, I wouldn't do that yet." Not long afterwards Benjamin excused himself as unfortunately he had to leave the cafe, because he was busy that day and had other errands to run. I believed that he would probably think about how best to assist me and advise me next time we met.

I did not want to be idle in my efforts to prove that the woman I loved was trying to kill me, and I poured over the available information. I wanted to double check everything and so I confirmed that my wife had purchased fuel at the service station, by checking our joint bank account statement at a local branch of the bank. I thought that maybe in this evidence of my wife's past must exist something that can be used against her, but the longer I examined the evidence the more it seemed that she had been very careful to hide her intentions for a long time.

I weighed up all the circumstantial evidence and solid facts that existed and I concluded that, based on the Australian legal systems principle that guilt has to be established beyond a reasonable doubt. I had to have something more concrete to ensure that I could get the police to act and ensure a conviction against the woman I loved that wanted me dead.

My wife was clearly sticking to her legal right not to say anything that would incriminate her and she was smart enough not to leave a trail of bread crumbs that would lead me to solid evidence where I could have her thrown in a jail cell and forgotten for the remainder of her miserable life.

I had deduced that my wife's motive has to be money. I only had evidence that was largely circumstantial that wasn't enough to ensure a safe conviction. In Australia, she would most likely be found not guilty of the crime of attempted murder on circumstantial evidence alone and I was in imminent danger until she was locked up. It is suffice to say that now, I knew this horrible knowledge about my wife that it did have an adverse effect on the amount of trust I now had in her. I did begin to withdraw sightly from her, by no longer telling her things and having shorter conversations with her, as the fear of her killing me was ever present.

Although my wife's motive and actions is evidence of her evil plan to kill me it simply was not enough to get police help.

I knew that I would have to change my Last Will and the life insurance policies beneficiaries to exclude the evil cold hearted bitch that pretends to be my loving wife. I read the statistical fact about homicides committed by women where 80% of women convicted of murder had killed their husbands or intimate acquaintances. This translates to my situation that if my wife was the evil killer I believe she may possibly be, then I have an 80% possibility of being her victim.

Now to return to the almost more important question of, if I am to be assassinated by my wife or just murdered by my wife. I rang the New South Wales Police Force Homicide Squad's Police Inspector, and I asked how important a person has to be for their murder to be an assassination. He said that according to the police every murder is a murder and they do not classify any murder as an assassination. I know that police have work to do but I can tell you that that telephone conversation was not pleasant for me, and that maybe the police force should only promote people with a more pleasant disposition. I suppose what I'm trying to say he was a rude asshole in a nice way, but I'm struggling with the words.

I then rang the Head Quarters of the Australian Federal Police and spoke with a staffer assigned to the Commissioners office. The Australian Federal Police do not classify any persons murder, no matter how important they are, as an assassination. The staffer explained that it is the media who generally term an important person's murder as an assassination. That was a very pleasant conversation and I was grateful for their information and advise.

I really wanted an answer to the pressing question of if my unnatural death at the hands of my killer wife will be remembered as me being assassinated or murdered so, I rang a friend of mine who works at a major newspaper and asked, "am I important enough that if I was murdered by say a lone gunman, would the newspaper report it as an assassination?" My friend laughed and said, "if they shoot you from a book repository or a grassy knoll then I would say yes" and then explained that we would have to finish the conversation later as he was very busy and his deadline was drawing nearer.

Later that night, my reporter friend telephoned me and he said that given my life and profile he thinks that the paper would just report me as being murdered unless I was somehow more famous. He also agreed that his newspaper were a bunch of leftist feel good nobodies and they wouldn't know a good story if they fell over it.

Like I would expect from any good reporter, his curiosity got the better of him and wanted to know why I would ask such a morbid question. I told him my tale from start to finish and all he could say was, "mate, I can feel the hair on the back of my neck standing up as I listen to you." I know exactly what it is like to feel the hair on the back of your neck tingle with every tick of the clock as I have been minutes away from death at the hands of my would be assassin wife. He composed his thoughts and said, "mate this is big and I have known you since school so I know your not lying, this is big."

I was now intrigued to know if I was important enough, or if my life achievements were enough that my murder would be called an assassination, so I asked my excellent Barrister and my researcher Benjamin to comment with honesty when we met for lunch about a week after my conversation with my reporter friend. I think it was my excellent Barrister who said, "your important to us, I just don't think that assassination would best describe a spousal killing. I see assassination as a murder committed against a political leader, a high government official or a person who is internationally known or high profiled," Benjamin agreed and added, "if your wife had you killed by someone else in a conspiracy and your murder took place at a public venue then maybe, why are you so obsessed with this?"

As a small side note at this time, I always type up a quick draft of my novel's and ask some people to read these and give me some feedback. This way I know if it's worth continuing with the story or going to watch my favorite strippers at the gentleman's club. During the first reading of this great novel a foot note was added by one of these readers that wrote;

"In this chapter, your story flaps around in the breeze and makes no sense, your way off track here and needs a total rewrite to concentrate on the subject of motive, consider scrapping half or more of this chapter."

Gee, some people are just hard to please when they are reading this grand novel about how my wife is trying to get away with my murder and how the entire thing has played out. Moving on from the distraction and harsh comment of this amateur critic and getting back on track to the motive of my wife to kill me.

Summing up in a simple sentence, to please the hard critics of this awesome tale of treachery, attempted murder and self preservation;

"I have deduced that my wife's motive for trying to kill me is money. $3,003,500 cash to be exact."

CHAPTER 4

THE GARDEN OF DEATH

Having survived two real attempts on my life and living with the next Australian black widow killer, my life began to settle down a little. Although, I did not falter on my vigilance at all as I wanted to survive and protect my children from having to live without such an awesome and loving father.

In early February 2017, I was doing some garden maintenance in the backyard of my home. It is often said that gardening gives a person a sense of satisfaction and is peaceful, they are very much wrong in my household. I was weeding around a tree in my backyard and I noticed that the tree was the poisonous Oleander that has long been associated with scorned wives poisoning their husbands. "She could use this tree to kill me!" I said to myself.

The use of Oleander poison continues in many societies, on the 9th September 2000, a woman named Angelina Rodriguez killed her forth husband using Oleander poison in his tea and sports drink in California, USA. Oleander is an easily obtained substance for a woman, with a proven history of successfully ridding women of their loving husbands.

I borrowed my neighbors petrol powered chainsaw, and I felt the testosterone running through my body as I cut the tree down and even dug out its roots to protect myself from any temptation that my wife could develop in the near future to poison me with this tree. I examined all the other plants in our back garden and soon came to the realization that I was living in a house surrounded by poisonous plants.

I was living in a garden of death.

I photographed every plant on my premises and spent many hours at the local library identifying and researching them all. How I had survived to date, living in this garden of death is not explainable and in many ways a modern miracle. I'm not saying the Catholic Pope is going to canonize me in the future for the miracles I have performed surviving so long, however, I am saying that I must be the most indestructible husband in Sydney with what I have lived through to date with the attempts on my life from my want to be black widow killing wife.

I identified a plant using the internet that is called Cerbera Odullam that was planted right beside our vegetable patch. I found myself gripped with fear once again, that I would soon be a homicide victim as I read that this plant is known by its more common name as "the suicide plant." I found an article on the internet that claimed the suicide plant is responsible for more deaths then any other plant in the entire world. This plant was right beside my vegetables and at any time my wife could have picked the plant and used it to kill me and claimed an innocent accident. Innocent, now there was a word that didn't describe my wife correctly.

I read an excellent article I found on the internet on the daily news website. It was dated on the 26th November 2004, by James Randerson, titled *Suicide Tree Toxin is Perfect Murder Weapon*. The article describes how Cererba Odollam is used by more people to commit suicide then any other plant. It also mentions how doctors, pathologists and coroners are failing to detect how often it is used to murder people.

"The perfect murder weapon" the words made me shake with realization that at any time my wife could have simply put the kernels of this plant in a curry or a stew to kill me. She may even have gotten away with it, given the use of this plant in Australia is so rare and not part of the normal toxicology examinations that are undertaken by coroners when determining the cause of a persons death.

I asked myself, "had she given up the idea of poisoning me with my food, or had I discovered the means that she was going to employ in her newly foiled plot?" The very moment I got home, I quickly changed my clothes and fetched my shovel to dig this evil plant out of my garden.

I also identified another evil and dangerous plant that was located just near my little garden shed, where I frequent. I store some tools and it is where I have my beer home brewing equipment. The poisonous plant is called Gastrolobium Bilobum, it is a nice looking heart shaped Australian native shrub that is used to make the super toxic poison known as 1080.

1080 is the horrendous toxic poison used to kill rabbits, wild dogs, feral pests and foxes in rural Australia. It is considered the only substance available to farmers and land owners in Australia, that allows them to kill almost any feral or pest animal and bird. This highly poisonous Australian native plant was growing in my garden, and I could not find a reasonable or legitimate reason as to why such a plant would be growing there. I kept thinking that my wife must have wanted the plant for its most evil use.

It is easy to understand my fear that my life was again in immediate and grave danger, when such plants are in my back garden and my homicidal loving wife has free and unhindered access to the poisonous plants.

My wife had only to walk into the back garden and pick herself a poesy of poison, without the fear of being seen by anyone due to the privacy design of our backyard garden. I disposed of every poisonous plant on my premises, and even took the bags of the vegetation to the council waste disposal depot to ensure my wife could not harvest the plants poison before the garbage is collected.

I found myself in the middle of a very large dilemma, on one hand I should report this black widow killer to the police and save my own life, then on the other hand my friends and family were telling me that my beautiful and caring wife is not trying to kill me.

I rang my researcher Benjamin and explained to him the latest evidence that I had gathered. I asked Benjamin, "why would this evil bitch have all these poisonous plants in our back garden if she didn't intend them for their evil abilities?" Benjamin is the consummate investigator and he replied, "mate, why did you have them? You live there also."

Benjamin was right again and it made me realize that I had to take immediate and decisive action to protect myself from being assassinated by the very person who vowed in the presence of God, in his church, to love me until death do us part. As I thought of those words, it made me realize that there may have been another possibility. That she wanted me dead because she had stopped loving me, and her freedom could only be allowed by her religious convictions if I was dead. My researcher Benjamin made a very valid point when he stated, "having a poisonous plant doesn't prove murderous intentions, it simply means you had poisonous plants in your backyard the same as three quarters of this country."

My friend Andy told me, "your more then slightly paranoid, your going fucking nuts, your wife ain't trying to murder you." I initially thought that my wife must had somehow manipulated Andy like she must have all of our other family and friends, then I remembered that she didn't like him very much and only spoke to him because she liked his wife Jackie.

I spoke to my friend Adam Davis about the newly discovered plant evidence I had uncovered and he asked;

"Were the plants already there when you brought the house? If they were already there, wouldn't that mean she didn't plant them to kill you?"

Two very valid and relevant questions indeed, and in one simple sentence. To answer the first question, "I simply do not know if they were there or if she planted them to kill me." I replied to his second question, "even if she didn't plant them, it doesn't mean she was not intending to use the vegetation's poisonous properties to murder me." I explained to Adam, that my wife has access to the internet and could have easily identified the poisonous plants the same as I did. Adam remained skeptical about the discovery of the poisonous plants.

I explained to my cousin Mick, "one of these poisonous plants are used to kill millions of animals every year in Australia. The Oleander has been used to kill many hundreds of men with the misfortune of being married to an evil woman, and let us not forget the one that is called the fucking suicide plant, that has killed literally millions in both suicide and murder." Mick did admit that there appeared to be a strange mixture of poisonous plants in one place, but would not commit himself to acknowledging that my darling wife was an evil and cold hearted killer.

It is undeniable that my wife has spent many hours tending to the garden and she has stated on many occasions, that she did enjoy picking the fresh home grown vegetables to use in her sometimes very bland cooking. I had clearly been close to death for some time, and needed to take drastic action to prevent my murder taking place.

My cousin Mick commented, "your wife's cooking isn't bland, why did you say it was?" and I quickly replied, "you obviously didn't taste her ratatouille with eggs that she made last night." Mick was still not convinced of the evil bitches treachery and her imminent plot to kill me. Mick suggested to me, "why don't you ask her if the plants were already there and if they were then you can relax, if she planted them then get the fuck out of there!"

I sat on my veranda and considered all of my options on how best to deal with this situation, without looking like I am insane or a paranoid person. I already knew that I was not a sufferer of the mental condition known as paranoid personality disorder or anything similar to that. I am sure that she is the only person trying to kill me right now, I also know I am not insane as I still function quite normally in every part of my life and that included my domestic situation. I am sure that if I was to walk into a police station right now, that they would not take me seriously as my family and friends kindly pointed out constantly.

It was my very grounded and understanding cousin Mick who said back in 1992;

"women are strange, one minute they love you and the other they want to skin you alive"

I never knew exactly what he meant when he said this until this very moment. I find myself stuck living with a crazed homicidal manipulative black widow killer. Other then divorce, I can see no other way out of this situation. Before I pack my bags and leave, I needed to know for sure if what I knew was real or if she was truly innocent. I didn't know what would happen to my children if I did leave her. Would this evil woman turn her murderous ways towards my children? This is a risk I could not take lightly and needed overwhelming evidence myself before I took any drastic actions.

I considered restricting access to our backyard for my wife and this was rejected very quickly. She needed access to hang out the clothes on the line, and to supervise the children when they are playing outside. I am not the type of man who would treat his wife more like a slave then a wife.

I also considered installing a fence to restrict access to the areas where I had found the poisonous plants, but again I was forced to reject this because it would make me seem paranoid with people and only serve to upset my wife more with me then she already is. Let's face it she wants me dead so she is very, very upset with me already.

I concluded that the only logical answer was to fully remodel the backyard, that way she could not plant poisonous plants in the yard again. I told my wife that I wanted to change the entire backyard, so we can make room for a swimming pool in the future when the kids are older. I was very cautious, to not give away the fact that I had discovered she had been nurturing enough poisonous plants to take out half of the population of the Eastern suburbs of Sydney.

My loving wife decided that I was right, *(something that just never happens and so heightened my suspicions)* and approved the change of our back garden and make many landscaping changes. She watched a home improvement TV show, and after thirty five minutes of viewing pleasure she was an expert landscape designer. My wife, the one who loves me more than air, designed our new backyard on a single piece of A4 paper using our kids colored pencils. Included was a list of plants that she selected from an internet page of a local plant nursery. Don't fear I double checked that list of plants very carefully and made sure they were all non poisonous.

A weekend in June was selected as the big day to undertake the work. I could not get my wife to understand that you cannot dig up a backyard, construct a new garden and plant it all out in a single day like they do on television. I hired a small machine to do all the heavy work and had a large skip bin delivered to dispose of all the rubbish. This was a major project and my wife promised to supervise every step of the way in the most nagging manner that she could, to ensure I worked hard with zero pressure and frustration.

A few days after starting the project, it was time to start planting the garden beds out with the fine selection of plants my wife had purchased. I am allergic to bee stings, so if I am stung by a bee I become a dead man walking. To my horror I had overlooked the dangers associated with some of these plants. My wife had purchased, with my approval of course, a number of flowering native non poisonous greivillia trees and many non poisonous flowering shrubs.

I had traded her garden of death full of poisonous plants for her to use to commit the most treacherous and heinous crime against me, for a garden that will increase my chances of being killed by a bee by thousands of a percentile. I said softly to myself "she is good, this bitch is going to have bees kill me and she wouldn't even be suspected of anything."

I had allowed myself to be manipulated into making the garden that will be my own demise. She had made me believe that I was changing the yard to save my own life, and all the time she was making it near impossible to prove that she had engineered my death.

I was living in a type of hell with the hour of my death lurking around me. I was trapped in a world where I knew my unpleasant death would come soon and was designed by my own wife and the mother of my children.

I recalled of the words of Field Marshal Sir Thomas Blamey, GBE,KCB, CMG, DSO, ED when he said;

"if you are faced with death, then killing the enemy is the only option you have."

Of course he was talking about soldiers waging battle in war time and I am talking about the imminent murder of myself, but it is all relevant. I knew that I had to do something to ensure my wife cannot get away with my murder.

If I killed my wife then no one would believe the circumstances that it was kill her or she kills me. Somehow I knew that she had just check mated me in the ultimate deadly game that she is playing. The clock of my doom was ticking down to the fate chosen by the heavens of my horrible death and my wife was going to get away with my murder.

I planted the plants according to my wife's design and instructions, I knew that she would check the plants to her plans. The garden looked great and even I thought it was more art then a garden, but it was a garden of death and she had to be stopped. That night I pretended that I was putting a liquid sea weed fertilizer on the new plants, instead I sprayed a strong herbicide onto the entire garden. Over the next few weeks these bee attracting killer plants would all be reduced to dead twigs, but more importantly I will be alive and well.

My unsuspecting wife would never know how I foiled her evil plot once again to kill me in a staged accidental anaphylaxis death. I felt almost a sense of pride as I watched the plants die slowly, and listened to my wife's complaints about the quality of the plants she had purchased from the local plant nursery. In this instance I had again saved my own life and felt like the road runner in the old cartoon that lived to tell his little tale another day. Together my wife and I purchased more Cestius Gallus friendly plants, that are not poisonous nor bee attracting from a different store. I added this latest saga to the seemingly endless tales of how my wife is trying to kill me at every opportunity.

I was discussing the garden of death with my brother in-law who said, "hang on! If my sister wants you dead, why wouldn't you be dead already?" As if to suggest that if I was right, then she would have already killed me and the fact I was still alive is evidence that she is not trying to kill me. He was in a way admitting that his sister, and my loving wife, was a stone cold killer that could take me out whenever she wanted. My fear is only growing and I cannot help to dwell on my fate.

CHAPTER 5

THE ANCEDOTAL EVIDENCE STACKS UP

Anecdotal evidence is one that is generally considered circumstantial in nature and the more I considered the happenings between 2015 and 2017, the more I realized that there may have been other numerous attempts for my wife to design my death. I do not consider these events as a direct attempt to assassinate me however, these other attempts against my life have to be included to properly convey the living hell and constant vigilance required to stay alive that I had lived with since 1995.

My wife, with the benefit of hindsight, had made many attempts to design my death by creating situations where the risk of accidental death is significantly greatly higher to me. Especially when a person has almost no handyman skills like your most favorite author.

Designing a persons death is different to conspiracy to commit murder, as that requires a person to plan and speak with another to murder a person. Attempting to murder a person is different to designing a murder, as attempting is to actually make an attempt by action that will end the life of another person by unnatural means.

I am alleging that my wife has actively designed my death by creating situations that were inherently dangerous, even for trained professionals and where there was the strongest possibility that I would die while undertaking tasks that were demanded to be undertaken by my super villain. I was trapped in a living hell where constant vigilance was the answer to my survival.

My wife was behaving like a super villain in the old comic books that I used to read as a child. I still expect her to walk out of our bedroom any day dressed in a costume and declaring me her arch nemesis, before unleashing a horde of minions on me. My life has been like the many good guys in a comic strip that are constantly battling a nemesis super villain and foiling their evil plots. I asked my children in my serious voice if I could be a super hero and they both replied words to the effect of, "nah, your too fat." I found an excuse to send the monsters to their rooms for thirty minutes as part vengeance and part punishment.

Cestius Gallus, the people's champion, is as useless as tits on a bull when it comes to being a handy man. I'm sorry that I have just destroyed the image you have of me as a handsome and romantic man that can put his hand to anything successfully. But it's true, I'm no handyman in anyone's eyes. I may be indestructible, handsome and adorable but like all men I have a fault and mine is I am not handy with maintenance and repairs. It's a deep shame that I have carried my entire life.

As an example of the level of my below average handyman abilities, I once tried to hang a lovely oil painting in my lounge room that I had been given by a very artistic fan of my true crime novels. The painting was their interpretation of what one of the persons described in one of my books would actually look like *(incidentally the painting was very close to their actual looks)*. I accidentally placed a very small 15cm wide hole in the wall when I missed the hook with the hammer I was using and struck the wall with some considerable force.

A very embarrassing event and one that my loving wife enjoyed telling to the plasterer and his young apprentice when they arrived to repair the hole in the wall. She also enjoyed telling the elderly handyman she hired, to place a simple hook in the wall to hang the painting that I was totally capable of doing. I realized that I was regularly emasculated by my wife for not being more handy around the house, and for not having the abilities of trades people that study for years to learn their craft.

I had just returned from hard work or interviewing and having coffee with another retired and definitely corrupt New South Wales Detective, when my loving wife demanded that I change into my old work clothes and install a new outside light at the front door. It seems that my wife, had visited a local lighting store and purchased a steel bunker style light that would give a nice industrial look to the front veranda without loosing any illumination for security.

In Australia each State has legislated the electrical industry, because of the dangers involved in working with or around electricity. It is illegal in all of Australia for a non qualified person to conduct electrical work of any kind. The cost of a qualified electrician is around $45 an hour, unless they are trying to rip you off. My loving beautiful wife, is fully conversant with such laws and the relatively low costs of hiring an electrical tradesman.

According to the joint Australian Institute of Health Welfare and Flinders University study on electrical injury and death published in 2007, around 1,493 people were hospitalized for injuries involving electricity in a two year period between 2002 and 2004. 162 people died from these injuries in the same time period. When you consider these figures and include my very low skill level for working with electrical equipment, I was a dead man walking for sure. I felt a strange sensation come over me that I had felt once before in my life, just before men with evil intent made an attempt to harm me when I worked in the New South Wales prison system. I knew that this woman that I loved, and who is the mother to my children had designed my imminent death by electricity.

I took the only course of action that was available to me, I refused her evil demand and I asked her, "why would you suggest that I play with electricity, is this an attempt to kill me and make it look like a household accident?" My wife became like an angry polar bear and screamed, "I just want you to change the fucking light fitting, oh my God how hard could it be?" and at that she stormed off into the house and refused to talk to me for about three hours.

Her silence could only be interpreted as an attempt to manipulate me into participating in her evil plot to kill me and make it look like an accident. I whispered to myself,"if it's so fucking easy why don't you do it, bitch!" and secretly I hoped that she didn't hear me to avoid the Hulk type behavior and response, that would follow such a comment coming to her attention. *(it's not being a coward when your wife is prone to violent outbursts and you believe that she is trying to murder you)*

Later that day I contacted a local electrician who agreed to come to my house on his way home and install the light. When the electrician arrived he confirmed that it is extremely dangerous for unqualified people to work on electrical equipment or wiring as they could die. He took about five minutes to change the light and charged me $50 for his expertise and time. Money very worth while spending to stay alive and well. This licenced electrician explained to me that;

"you can't see or smell electricity, it is so much more dangerous to work with and kills easily"

As I watched television later that night, I was hiding my anger and it was like a kettle being heated on the stove top inside me just waiting to boil over. I asked my wife to join me on the lounge to talk, and she made me wait forty six minutes before she sat beside me. That forty six minutes my wife made me wait, was a bigger mistake then her attempt to kill me by forcing me to illegally work on the deadly electrical wiring of our house.

The sly, evil black widow killer sat down, then crossed her arms and had a type of hurry up look on her face just like a teenager who is being told their choice of friends is not appropriate. I did something that I now regret and I am fully aware is not the correct manner to deal with such situations. I just exploded, I couldn't stop myself from shouting and blurting out the most hurtful and strong words I had ever used with my loving and darling wife.

My memory is a little vague on the exact wording of the heated conversation, but if you were to ask my wife she would want you to believe that she sobbed for an hour after being hurt by the man she loves as he abused her for no good reason. Of course that is total nonsense as everyone knows that based on the evidence provided so far, any tears displayed by this cunning evil rat would be fake.

"I had again made my wife a woman scorned."

The stark realization that my wife had designed my unnatural death by attempting to manipulate me to play with a households most dangerous essential utility, would make a lesser man cry!

In January 2017, my wife's cunning and simple plan to design my death by misadventure or household accident increased. I live in a two story brick veneer house in the eastern suburbs of Sydney. Those who are familiar with the region, would know that house owners wage a constant war against blocked gutters and falling leaves from the endless large trees in the region.

I had just finished washing the car and I walked inside the house to make a coffee and take a well deserved break. I became aware of the presence of my wife standing behind me and she stated in an abrupt and forceful manner, "you have to clean out the gutters today, I'm sick of waiting, DO IT TODAY."

To work at a height over two meters in Australia,

you are required special personal protective equipment for safety and to prevent workplace death. The government's of most modern societies have placed rules, regulatory framework and mandatory training in place to prevent deaths from heights as it is a large concern for the construction industry.

In October 2013, Safe Work Australia issued the publication *Work-Related Injuries and Fatalities Involving a fall from Height*. I remember reading the document and was surprised to learn that such is the dangers of working from heights, that Safe Work Australia describe falls from heights as;

"a major cause of death and serious injury in Australian workplaces"

In the interest of accuracy and to be fair to my future widow, the risks of death from a fall in Australia is only about a quarter of a percent per one hundred thousand workers. Shockingly of all the workers killed by fall related injury, it was males in my age group that made up 70% of those who died. Statistically, I was more likely to die then if I sent my young daughter up the ladder with a brush and a hose, if I could trust her to do a proper job then I would have considered sending her up the ladder in my place.

I knew what was going on right then and there, my

wife knew I was tired and possibly fatigued from washing the car and working while fatigued is the same as working drunk.

The New South Wales government once ran a television campaign that said driving fatigued was the same as driving drunk. My evil future murdering wife, demanded that when in a state akin to being drunk, I climb to the second story roof of my house on a ladder without any personal protective equipment or fall restraint device and bend over the edge and clean gutters with water that would increase the risk by making the surface slippery. I was dead if I agreed to this evil plot.

I cringed with her demand and I took off to the lounge room and quickly found myself doing online internet searches. I finally found a local professional to come and clean the gutters out and ultimately saving myself, being the next statistical death in Safe Work Australia's next publication. The professional arrived the next morning and he wore a special harness, he installed some temporary cables that would protect him if he fell off the roof and he said, *"mate, even with all this fall protection, it's bloody dangerous, you did the right thing calling us and not just climbing up there yourself."* I was very happy that my cunning wife, who had obviously designed my accidental fall to death was within hearing of the professional gutter cleaner. I still did not dare look at her in some type of attempt to pacify the darkness that existed inside her.

Later that night while I joined my cousin Mick at our favorite gentleman's club, where we watched Amber do her pole dancing routine. I told him about the gutter cleaning event and how close I had became to dying by a fall related injury. Mick validated my thoughts and feelings and said, "if you had climbed that ladder and tried to get the gutters clean, then your chance of death is almost fifty, fifty!"

He then explained that he came to the percentage conclusion by estimating the number of houses in the region and the number of times the homeowners clean out their gutters. He compared that with the percentage of people doing that type of work, that die per one hundred thousand workers and then added my age to the equation. Look it made perfect sense at the time and let's leave it at that. We both agreed over a few alcoholic beverages, that half of the time I climb the ladder to the roof of my home I would statistically be guaranteed to die. Trust me I'm sure that the mathematics are right.

In March 2017, I was again banging the big drum that my wife is trying to get away with my murder to my friend Michael. He has had to listen to this stuff for many years now, and he has resigned himself to listening to me bang this drum for at least five minutes every time we talk. It was Michael who reminded of the event where Michael and his wife met both myself and my wife in the city for dinner. We were all walking back to our cars after a fantastic meal at 34BIA restaurant in the inner city suburb of Redfern. There was a homeless man that stank of body odour and faeces that was sitting against a fence along the pathway, and he stared at my wife intensely as we walked towards our cars.

Without notice or provocation the homeless man screamed at my wife, "you have a shadow on your soul, a dark shadow on your soul." Michael jokingly remarked, "maybe that homeless guy knew something that we didn't." I had forgotten this homeless guy until Michael reminded me of it. There is some people who believe that others can see people's auras, and they are more attuned to the aspect of the source which to me is one the many mysteries of the universe that I do not generally subscribe too.

At Orebro University located in Sweden a study was performed where they compared the eyes of 428 people with their personality traits, to see if their eye structure reflected the character of the people. The researchers put forth their theory that eye structure and personality could be linked because the genes responsible for development of the eye, also play a role in the development of the frontal lobe of the brain, which influences personality.

Some people have proposed the hypothesis that people can read the eyes of a stranger and identify the person's character, without knowing why they are usually correct about the character assumptions they make by simply looking into the eyes of another person.

Just days ago this theory would have had zero merit with me unless the homeless man was tested under strict scientific conditions by experts. However, given the evidence against my wife and her black widow character, I now believe that this man has been gifted with the ability to read the character of my wife by simply looking at her eyes. It is plausible that the homeless man believes he is looking into a person's soul when he is actually identifying their character.

Sitting in my home office where I have been typing this novel or more correctly described as where I have been recording the accurate events leading to my murder. I noticed on the 4th of March 2017, that some time between 9:20am and 10:15am (when I was out of the home office) that my loving and caring wife had placed an air freshener on the top shelf beside my Colin McCarthy award. The air freshener delivers a timed dose of fragrance air into the room and it had a powerful smell of vanilla.

Every bloody time this thing delivered its scent into the small home office environment, I would immediately get a headache from the overpowering smell of its artificial vanilla scent. I thought that it was possible that the device was designed for a larger area of space then what we were using it for, so I downloaded the manufacturers material safety data sheet or MSDS as it is universally known as.

I am surprised the neighbors living next door didn't complain about the sound of the alarm bells going off in my head, they were that loud as I read the deadly ingredient of this cancer causing death trap. My wife had been at it again and this time she had designed the best way to kill off her husband, without any suspicion falling onto her. The air freshener included the ingredient formaldehyde. Formaldehyde is a highly toxic substance and known carcinogen and phenol which causes hives, convulsions, circulatory collapse, coma and even death.

The air freshener was designed by the manufacturer to be used in an area almost a hundred and twenty times the space of my home office. This means that I was breathing in a dose that was a hundred and twenty times the dose that makes the substance relatively safe, given its deadly contents. My evil black widow, cold hearted bitch of a wife had now designed my death by cancer. The deadly ingredient of this can of death, would infect my body and cause me to die of cancers such as lung cancer, throat cancer or even brain cancer.

This cannot be a coincidence, that the air freshener is a can of death with a pretty label and my wife has an alleged history of trying to kill me. "Enough is enough," I yelled and took the air freshener down and threw it into the adjoining kitchen where she was standing while she made herself a coffee *(another valid point that should be mentioned, she makes herself coffee and hardly asks me if I want one).* "your games up woman! I've put up with this shit for long enough, no more!" I screamed, as I considered how close she had come to killing me off with a can of her deadly air freshener. My wife is a very patient woman, as demonstrated by how long she has been trying to murder me. I am fully aware that she must hate me because again she has been trying to murder me for many years, so it is reasonable that her reaction was not unexpectedly very angry and boarder line violent.

"You fucking moron, why did you throw that at me! What is your fucking problem now dickhead?" I recall vividly that was the opening statement that commenced the next twenty minutes of sailor talk from my wife, and it left me in total fear of the black widow killer that lurked inside her.

I thought;

"shit, I've done it now. I have now made my wife, a woman very very scorned".

After her twenty minutes of solid emasculating abuse, my ever loving wife then spent the next hour reminding me of any small thing I had done to annoy her in the last twenty plus years. I find it amazing that she could not remember to buy me a bottle of scotch when she was at the shops yesterday, but she can remember every minor bad thing I have done in the past twenty plus years.

I knew that her attempts to design my death had to stop! So I did the impossible I said, "listen you black widow bitch, I'm taking this to the cops. I have survived every one of your murderous attempts and now it ends, your a fucking low life killer."

Yes, I actually said it and exactly those very words. I then watched with a heavy heart as she proceeded to pack an overnight bag for me and throw my ass out until as she stated, "you get some fucking help, you stupid fucking moron."

Regrettably, I didn't save the can of death disguised

as a harmless air freshener as evidence. I took my little bag of clothes and drove to my friends house for the night as I considered what to do next.

My wife had telephoned Dr Sukit and discussed the event. She pretended that she didn't know why I had thrown the can of death at her, and she also pretended that she had no idea what the argument, (that she was the major player in) was even about. She had Dr Sukit ring me and I listened to him intently and simply said, "Doctor, thank you for your call, I will ring the evil bitch when I get home from Thailand" and I hung up. "Two can play at that game" I said to my friend and I went to bed and had the deepest and longest sleep I had in years, safe from assassination at the hands of the wife of your greatest true crime author.

Over the next few days I was able to reconcile the incident with my wife. After admitting that I was wrong and she was right, that I am dumb and she is smart. After admitting that she is beautiful and I am ugly and that I love her, she accepted my apology and admitted me reentry into our matrimonial home that I reluctantly accepted only to be better placed to protect my children and gather evidence of my loving wife's evil plot.

Further anecdotal evidence hides in plane sight. I Have built a solid reputation with my loyal readers as Australia's greatest true crime author, it will surprise even my biggest fans that I have some vices. I am addicted to the taste and habit of smoking cigarettes and cigars. There is almost nothing about actual smoking that I do not enjoy. I most certainly do not enjoy the endless restrictions on smokers in Australia, I also do not enjoy being told by a nagging wife that I cannot smoke on the veranda when the children are playing or sitting around me. My wife regularly nags at me, "I don't want the kids to breath in your filthy second hand smoke."

My loving and caring wife, who I am sure that every reader would now agree has waged a secret war against me to end my life in the most unnatural manner that she can, has never asked me to cut down or stop smoking. My wife is aware that cigarettes are cancer causing death sticks and yet she has never been concerned for my health or well being, only for our children.

I suspect on reasonable grounds, that my wife is hoping that I get cancer and die so she can be blameless in my death and doesn't have to kill me herself. My wife regularly purchases me cigarettes and cigars, ensuring I have a plentiful supply at all times. She has even purchased me a nice large ash tray, a lovely Zippo brand lighter and a high end cigar cutter in encouragement of my smoking.

I know that some readers would be saying that I am clutching at straws mentioning my wife's indifference to my smoking and health, however this encouragement to my smoking demonstrates how she has zero concern to my health and longevity as her husband and the father to our children. How can she be so concerned for the well being of our children that I cannot smoke on the veranda when they are present. Yet she has been buying me a carton of cigarettes a week, and I'm not to form the opinion that she is hoping I get lung or throat cancer and die a horrible death in a palliative care ward of our local hospital.

Her cunning plan in designing my death knows no boundaries, and yesterday as I sat typing up this champion novel I decided that I would quit smoking for good and force her to come up with a new way of killing me. I told her, "honey, I'm going to quit smoking so don't buy me cigarettes next week." My wife exposed her hand and replied "oh, really! You know you get grumpy without smokes, are you sure?" I don't know how you take her reply, however it was evidence enough to me that she wants me to keep smoking and die.

Since 1995, I have had a great friend called Harry. She is a saint, a loyal friend and a great cook who specializes in traditional Italian cuisine. Harry is now 42 years old of Italian descent, and is married to a great guy who has model looks and a body that he claims makes him "eye candy for gay guys." I went to her house and had a very lovely brunch with her. Brunch is a very romantic meal, and one should be alert at all times to the advances of their brunching partner to ensure that the meal does not turn into romance.

I told the lovely Harry about all the anecdotal evidence that I have been writing about and she laughed at me and said, "yes, take it to the police that she is trying to kill you because she has never asked you to stop smoking and they will lock you up in a mental hospital."

I have always respected the advice of the lovely Harry and I replied, "I know that, but stacked with everything else isn't it something?" she simply told me, "Cestius, you know I have all the time in the world for you, but you have to admit that this is lame." I thanked the lovely Harry for her advice and I decided to include my wife's encouragement to my smoking in this champion novel as anecdotal evidence anyway. I want to show the world how my evil black widow wife is happy for me to die any way at all, so long as I die.

CHAPTER 6

THE POLICE WILL NOT SAVE ME

With ever increasing suspicion that it was only a short matter of time before I was to be murdered by this evil, cold, black widow killer of a wife of mine. I decided to ignore the advice of all of my family and friends, and to walk into a police station and lay the evidence in front of a detective.

You must understand I was a corrections officer for a long time, and I have seen both good and bad police and the results that come from a bad police investigation. I am one of the ultimate skeptics when it comes to police and their abilities to do a simple job, I also hate rats, informants and dobbers. So it is very hard for someone like me, to conclude that the best course of action to take is to walk into a police station and speak to a bloody copper. The prisoners used to sing a song in the prison yard whenever a policeman would come into the jail for a visit, it was a stupid song that the only words were "all coppers are fucking cunts doodah, doodah." A very catchy song indeed and it sticks in your head for days.

Every responsible parent teaches their child that if you are scared or need help to call the police and they will do everything that they can to help you, sound advice that I have given my own children and so I decided to take my own advise and seek help from the police.

The experience of walking into a police station with an envelope that is crammed with evidence of repeated attempted murder, by the person you love and cherish more then anyone else in the world is quite difficult. Police stations in New South Wales are as welcoming as an portable toilet at a construction site.

It all starts with the clerical officer sitting behind the counter. In their wisdom, the police force has given the clerk enormous power to screen who you will talk with. The clerk will decide if you are important enough to see a detective or just ring some hotline, so no one has to deal with you.

After about thirty seconds, that included the standard greeting required to display good manners. The clerical officer did not consider why I wanted to speak with a detective important enough and suggested, "if you want to leave the envelope for one of them to look at, then I suppose that's alright."

I was quite shocked and asked, "do you mind if I write down your name ma'am? I want to make sure that everyone knows the name of the fuckwit who turned me away when I came to the police, with evidence of a murder that was going to place any time now." I then turned and walked out of Maroubra police station, and came to the realization that the police will not save me. I rang a Detective friend from outside the police station and he said, "mate, ring the Detectives office first and then she can get fucked." As I drove home deflated and sensing the black dog of depression walking beside me I thought;

"community policing is all bullshit, fuck these coppers, they get nothing from me from now on"

There is more then one way to skin a cat, is an old and meaningful saying that is used by every Australian. It means, that there is always another way to do something. I drove to the city and visited my excellent Barrister, and I changed my Last Will to exclude my wife in every way. I made copies of all the evidence to date and wrote a statement that was witnessed by my excellent Barrister *(I also included the name of the Maroubra police station clerical officer who turned me away just so her role isn't forgotten)*. I deposited certified copies with my excellent Barrister and later that day I sent the originals to my bank in Munich, Germany, where they were placed in my safe deposit box by a German lawyer I use now and then.

I said to myself, "what's the point of having a large network of police and law enforcement officers if you can't get them to help you with this." I then organized a meeting with two current Detectives that have assisted me with my awesome true crime novels. I set out the evidence in chronological order, and supported my allegations with a copious amount of documents.

The two detectives sat and listened to me without asking any questions at all, when I had finished my presentation one of the detectives said, "is that it, mate you have a dream, a car accident that you proved is a car accident, a fucking garden and her wanting you to clean a gutter, is this some type of joke?"

The meeting then just simply ended, the two Detectives swallowed their coffee and left with the most junior of the men saying;

"please don't waste our time with some shit like this, we thought you were working on something that was real, don't ring us unless it means an arrest."

It's incredible how you realize a person has only been dealing with you so they can somehow advance themselves. These two coppers have been contacting me and meeting for coffee now since I started writing my latest true crime novel. That's only because they wanted to make an arrest and advance their careers after I had done all the work. I vowed that these two key stone cops would never hear from me again.

It was my father who said;

"in life the most important thing to remember when dealing with police is that all coppers are arrogant and cunts."

Again, I sort the assistance of the police and again they turn me down and will not help me. The thoughts that I had to kill or be killed had started flooding back to me. The irony is, that if I did kill my wife to stop her killing me then the cops would happily arrest me for her murder, and yet they will not protect me from this evil black widow killer.

As a result I have now severed all contact with police in New South Wales, and I've vowed that I wouldn't help them ever again solve a crime as they seem to generally live up to what one the prisoners at Long Bay Jail once told me about them, "fucking all dogs and liars, that would fine their own Grandmothers for Jay walking and still expect to get an invite to Sunday lunch from her."

It is a very big blow to your self confidence and mental stability, when you are outright dismissed by the very people who are sworn and employed to protect you. I knew that my evidence was not an open and shut case, but it still needs a trained eye cast over it to see if it holds enough weight to warrant charges against the woman who appears to want me dead at any cost.

CHAPTER 7
ARE YOU FUCKING
KIDDING ME?

In the evening of 20ᵗʰ June 2017, I left my laptop computer turned on in my home office after a full day typing this world class novel. My wife must have sneaked into the home office and read the draft of this true tale of evil some time after I retired for the evening, and sat in the lounge room to interact with my children and watch some television. In the morning of the 21ˢᵗ June 2017, I found the following passages had been included in this novel by my wife.

Firstly, it is very rude to think that you can just touch another person's work laptop computer without their permission. This demonstrates the sneakiness and total disregard for my privacy that my wife shows. Secondly, in the interest of fairness and providing you with a balanced true tale I have included her passages, unedited, to demonstrate to you how evil and manipulative my wife is in her denials of the facts and truth, that I am willing to swear in a court of law.

Husband,

Are you fucking kidding me? I read this new book of yours last night. I hope that this book is some new type of writing that is fiction. I have not attempted and would not kill you! You are the love of my life and my soul mate and it hurts my heart that you have written such hurtful words. I think that you need some help, and hope dearly that you would work with Doc Oscar on your paranoia that seems to drive your feelings that I am trying to kill you. You call me such hurtful things in this book babe and describe me as evil, cunning, a black widow killer and make such horrible accusations against me. I just don't know what to think.

I am not responsible for those dreams that you used to have, that I was going to poison your food, why would I do such a thing? You are the father of our beautiful children, I want them to grow up with their father who is smart and kind. It now makes such sense to me how you always ate with the light on, and waited for me to sit at the table and start eating before you would. I used to think that you were being a gentleman, and now I think you were just waiting to see if I had poisoned your food. How hurtful. I really think that Doc Oscar can help you if you give him a chance. He likes you and you both have so much in common. So please let him help you get over this and rationalize your thoughts so you become the man you were before, the man that I fell in love with all those years ago.

The car accident was just a car accident. How can you think that I would try and kill you in a car accident that I was driving. I was in the car also and it was a simple car accident. I don't know how else to put it, why would I drive a car and roll it when I'm driving just to kill you. I know that you hit your head in the accident and we never had you checked out properly, but maybe it's time you visit the GP for an x-ray or something. You have not been yourself since then and it worries me greatly.

I love you so much and I would never try to kill you. I can't believe you thought you had to totally change the garden because we had some plants that are poisonous. Newsflash honey, this country is full of the most deadly things and just about every house in Australia has something that is deadly. You spent thousands of our savings changing the garden because you thought I could use a few plants to poison you. WTF?

I think that you need to speak with Doc Oscar this week, instead of going to the pub with your cronies. It pains me to beg you to get some help and I am here to support you every step of the way, the same as I have always been here to support you and love you with all of my heart.

When I asked you to change the light, and clean the gutters out I was never trying to kill you. I love you. I thought it was easy as Ben said it's a five minute job to change the light, and David next door cleans his gutters out in thirty minutes. If it is the case that you just didn't want to do it, then please don't make me your excuse. Please see it from my point of view, that my asking you to fix a light or clean the gutters was just to have the light fixed and gutters cleaned and not to kill you. I feel like I'm being attacked in this book of yours all the way through. The title is even how I'm trying to get away with your murder. Babe, please speak with Doc Oscar, I emailed him and he wants to talk with you.

When you threw the air freshener at me and you were screaming at me that I was trying to kill you, I didn't know what was wrong and thought that your PTSD was playing up again. I was scared because you were so angry at me, and I had no idea that it was about the silly smell of the air freshener and not at something I had done. If you were really worried about the chemicals, then why did you have the house sprayed for spiders and bugs every six months by Doug the pest controller? I'm sure that those chemicals are more dangerous then the air freshener.

We have to communicate better and you need to speak with Doc Oscar because, it was only an air freshener and all the other things are just you being paranoid. Babe, you worry me and I love you so much we can work through all this together and get you back on track.

Did you really go to the police? You hate the police, so I'm thinking you didn't but I'm not sure. I

HOPE THAT YOU DIDN'T BECAUSE I WILL NOT BE HAPPY.

Call Doc Oscar today.

Please do it for us Babe, I love you. -xxx-

....

Law enforcement and police officers interview people to cement them into a story that they then devote themselves to destroying. My wife had just made the largest mistake of her life by making a type of statement that detailed her denials.

Her statement is great evidence to collect and it was done without me even trying. Through her sneaky, conniving and underhanded illegal surveillance of my work laptop computer, my wife has now concreted herself into a version of events and denied her evil and provable intentions. My wife has clearly attempted to make me feel that I am paranoid, the person at fault and not the victim that I am.

This manipulative woman has even enlisted the assistance of Dr Oscar Sukit in her plot to make me believe that I am crazy, or in need of some type of psychological help. The facts and circumstances stand strong in the eyes of the justice system, and they scream out that my wife is an evil person who is motivated and concentrated on the murder of her husband for financial gain.

Reading her words, was like reading some illegible graffiti on the back of a public toilet door as she tried to make me think that I am insane. Her continued use of the word "love" sickened me, as I knew it was hatred and evil intentions that she harbored toward me and the flame of passion had long burnt out in her heart.

If Dr Oscar Sukit was here right now, I could only find the words "fuck you, you have allowed yourself to be manipulated by someone who you should have realized was working you!" I am sure that he will understand that I will not be using his services in my true crime novels anymore and no longer contacting him in any way.

With this new evidence written by my wife herself, it will be very hard for her to change her story and pretend that I was some form of abusive husband or she had a just reason to kill me when she finally murders me. I am positive that anyone who has read this awesome true story, would now be fully convinced of my wife's guilt.

Now that this novel has been written it is my sincere hope that it will halt my wife's constant attempts to murder me. Remember that she is trying to get away with my murder.

ABOUT THE AUTHOR
By Lincoln Houghton Esq

Cestius Gallus is a former highly decorated corrections officer, who had risen to the esteemed rank of Senior Correctional Officer in Sydney's Long Bay Jail and served for 10 years and 255 days. He now lives in Sydney's Eastern Suburbs with his wife and two children and is an award winning writer. Cestius Gallus cannot use his real name to protect his family from the criminal underworld and to prevent the police from harassing him for the identities of the persons in this book.

Cestius was awarded the prestigious Royale Institute for Education's Colin McCarthy award for his first published novel titled "The Greatest Prison Book Ever".

The first book in his true crime organization series "STAR The Most Successful Criminal Enterprise in Australia" has been nominated for numerous awards in 2017 and the contents of the book are part of ongoing international police investigations. Cestius Gallus exposed the crime organization and shocked the policing community at how successful they really were.

Cestius is generally considered the greatest crime author in Australia and one of the bravest men in Australia's history, Cestius Gallus has received numerous bravery commendations and medals. I have met the family of Cestius and now I know where he draws his strength and motivation for life from, they are very supportive, loving and his wife is a great cook and conversationalist.

Cestius lives a quiet life now and writes novels that are unique and tell a story that the public craves for and wants to know how things actually work. Cestius Gallus enjoys sitting and speaking with old criminals and corrupt cops and has planned to do many more books like no other author has or can.

Cestius writes in an easy to read manner and is often found sitting on the veranda of his home typing away at his novel. Cestius Gallus suffers from Post Traumatic Stress Disorder as a result of his correctional career and stills undergoes treatment. Writing novels has been an escape from the crippling effects of PTSD.

It is easy to argue that Cestius is the most romantic author in Australia, but to the literacy world he is always going to be an anonymous author with a weird pen name. Cestius enjoys the many fan emails and letters that he receives from readers and he keeps every one in a special place in his house. He is humbled by the feedback from his readers and hopes that you enjoy this book.

If you would like to email Cestius
cestiusgallus@gmail.com

he intrepidly awaits your emails.